Lean and Six Sigma Stories

Izzy Sanchez and Ian Cato

Lean and Six Sigma Stories by Izzy Sanchez and Ian Cato Published by Tactegra LLC 18Cabarrus Avenue West, Concord NC 28025

www.Tactegra.com

© 2018 Tactegra LCC

All rights reserved. No portion of this book may be reproduced in any form without permission from the publisher, except as permitted by U.S. copyright law. For permissions contact:

info@Tactegra.com

Cover by Tactegra LLC.

INTRODUCTION

"Six Sigma is not for us, lean works better than six sigma, six sigma is faster than lean, lean is faster than six sigma, lean takes too long, six sigma is too restrictive. "

These are many other variants we have heard over the years from people from all industries and backgrounds. Are they right? You bet, in their mind, based on their experience, and feelings, they are right. That's what they know. Very likely they have suffered by some poor implementation of lean, six sigma, or both, and have seen it fail, or have been brainwashed by someone claiming to be an expert in either one, or both. But more realistically they have been hurt by a one trick pony that tried to follow a book or got trained by someone who has no real-life experience in lean or six sigma.

This book is a group of short stories collected over our combined 60+ years of successes in lean and six sigma, in simple business language. Some stories are real, some may not be so real, you can decide while remembering "that real life is stranger than fiction". Business all over the world is very similar, and you may find that the stories are relatable to everyday life and activities.

So, if you have either embraced or rejected Lean Six Sigma, Continuous Improvement, or similar programs, you will enjoy the stories as they are from real engagements and projects, and who knows, you may see your very similar situation here….

ACKNOWLEDGMENTS

We would like to thank all of our mentors, clients, colleagues, and past supervisors that introduced us to the world of Continuous Process Improvement, Theory of Constraints, Lean, Six Sigma, Leadership Through Quality, Managing by Fact, Process Re-engineering, Red X, Statistical Process Control, Taguchi Methods, and many other disciplines throughout the years. The list of influencers is long and very distinguished and would merit a book onto itself. We have learned, grown, and expanded our practice and knowledge thanks to so many people who decided to take a chance on us early on our careers and later as we continue to perform as a consulting firm, dedicated to the never-ending progress of effective and efficient processes. To all, thank you for all the staunch support.

1. THE COUNTY ORDINANCE

Introduction:

Spoiler alert - creating a new or amended ordinance for a county government body is not an easy task. It requires thousands of hours of meetings, dozens of drafts, negotiations, compromises, political posturing, you name it. We're not going to focus on the latter however, but on the actual "process" of creating a county ordinance related to recycling of cardboard boxes in construction sites. We know, break out the Coronas and turn up the Kool and the Gang. But what follows is a fascinating glimpse into the application of Lean Six Sigma tools and how they can eliminate re-work, accelerate adoption, engage the community, and those the most affected.

How It Works Today:

The mandate:

"We need an ordinance for construction sites and large single events (fairs, festivals, etc.) to mandate the recycling of cardboard. It must be broken down and separated from all other waste."

When a county team responsible for drafting such ordinances receives the call, they first begin to review existing ordinances and then create a first draft with the aid of the legal department.

Next comes the socialization process, where the draft is presented to various groups for input and critique. This starts with industry groups, local chambers of commerce, small town leaders, and other groups in the area. The process is relatively simple, attending a meeting with the aforementioned groups. A notice may be posted and a line item in the agenda is created in the meetings to add "Proposed County Ordinance on Cardboard Recycling."

Feedback from the meetings varies, depending on constituency groups. Yet, every time county staff attends, they hope and knock on wood that the ordinance will be received without too much resistance and that they come out Ok. That's the way it's always been …

As time goes by, additional drafts are amended, questions and queries from external sources start to arrive, which in turn leads to subsequent changes and even more amendments.

Eventually, meetings are schedule with industry groups to present the reconstituted ordinance that now represents a significant amount of input and work. The industry group representatives then provide their input with changes/guarantees that the county must go back and update. These updates then need to go back to other groups for their feedback. Sound exhausting?

The ordinance continues down the same path until either time expires or it could pass a vote by the county commissioners. At the commissioners meeting, however, some will air current issues that they have been made aware by their constituents (industry or affected company owners) and request the county to go back and answer even more questions. Eventually, (at some point in time in the future) the ordinance will be passed, with probably four times the number of pages of the original intent, and with language only an attorney could appreciate.

From a Lean Six Sigma perspective, the process is a disaster. So, could there be a different way? What do you think ...

In The Near Future:

Remember the mandate:

"We need an ordinance for construction sites and large single events (fairs, festivals, etc.) to mandate the recycling of cardboard. It must be broken down and separated from all other waste."

The county team responsible for drafting such an ordinance gets the requirement, and begins to review existing ordinances for potential overlap. They then convene to create a charter, the first step in the Lean Six Sigma project.

The charter forces the team to draft a problem or opportunity statement. This exercise changes the perspective, as the team now creates "increase construction and event cardboard recycling by 100%." The goal and how the team will focus their energy is now very different - the ordinance is an outcome of the charter, not the driving force. This provides clarity of purpose and a numerical goal. Next, the team brainstorms on the questions they need answered, such as:

- How much is recycled today by construction and events?
- Who else does this and how do they do it?
- Is 100% too high, should we stagger the goal to lead up to 100%?

- Who's impacted by this goal?
- What are the potential barriers to the goal?
- What would the process look like for construction or events?
- What services should the county offer and what are the costs?

The team realizes they don't have an existing process to achieve the goal, so it seems like Design For Six Sigma (DFSS) will be the best methodology to use. This methodology aids in creating a process, considering the lean and six sigma principles. The path leads to the identification of customers, their needs/desires, and then designing a process to achieve the needs, testing it, and eventually rolling it out. But let's continue with the methodology, the ordinance will flesh its way out.

The team begins to identify their customers and who will most likely be impacted by the new ordinance and goal. At the forefront - construction firms and general contractors as they are critical to the goal's success. Next, large event planners, cities, and towns that will generate cardboard during unique events. Event sponsors and venues are included as they are instrumental in collecting the cardboard. The county waste management department, since they must deal with collections and the processing of the extra cardboard, and potentially less waste to landfill. Finally, subcontractors or haulers that may actually engage in the physical collection and delivery will be included. The team realizes there are others, such as county commissioners and town leaders who will have to vote on and potentially enforce the ordinance, so they are added on as additional stakeholders and key customers in the process.

With their "customers" (stakeholders) identified and segmented, the team creates a simple Stakeholder Analysis to ensure they capture the perspectives and expectations of each group. They begin by asking questions surrounding what needs to be done to "increase construction and event cardboard recycling by 100%." Now, let's read that statement again. Notice anything different? It's vastly different than the initial ordinance mandate.

The team uses that goal as a starting point and begins to select representative companies and individuals to interview. They will use the tools of Design for Six Sigma to capture, characterize, and quantify what are the needs, requirements, and concerns of each group. They then use an affinity method to see where and how they can intersect multiple needs with single "design specifications" that will be used to build the ordinance. That way the ordinance language will have provisions and answers to the issues which increases the probability of sailing it through.

Each group is segmented, and the team conducts one-on-one interviews and focus groups with construction companies, contractors, town and city leaders, enforcement organizations, event planners, waste management companies and recyclers. During one of these interviews with a small town supervisor, the gentleman inquired as to how many companies were being interviewed. The team lead quickly replied:

"Twelve is what we need for interviews, then three focus groups."

His reaction was a bit surprising as he responded, "that is not nearly enough, there are hundreds of companies to talk to and it doesn't feel right." The team stuck to the facts, replying that feelings aside, they are calculating the number of interviews and focus group needed based on statistical assurances of capturing the largest number of needs and issues, and any more would simply be a waste of resources.

Like most people who first hear this information, the gentleman was not convinced and thought the number of interviews must be based on the total number of companies to "feeeeel right." Again, feeeeelings. This is a perfect example where Lean Six Sigma can help answer questions based on facts (not feeeelings) and provide a high level of confidence that the outcome will be correct.

> "Have faith, we are using tried and true statistical models to obtain the true critical inputs."

During the interviews and focus groups the team collected a large amount of information in the form of transcripts and verbal data that was analyzed and segmented into common threads with small variations. Some of these were:

- How do you control recycling containers?
- What happens if other parties use the containers?
- Going to 100% is not feasible.
- Who is going to cover additional inspection costs?
- Too much cardboard generated on weekends won't get picked up, so storing it will be a problem.
- I can't control that everyone in my site will use the container.
- There is no space to add in another container.
- Folks will throw trash into container.
- Why should we do this? I don't see the benefit.
- We can't process the extra work.
- Our drivers don't work weekends.
- We can't do it, we're too small.

Most of the comments were attributed to the expected lack of control they would have with the new cardboard containers, and the potential mixing of cardboard and waste due to carelessness or lack of knowledge.

After dissecting all the information retrieved (literally thousands of comments), and combining them into key categories and common needs, the team ended up with the following list of key needs and requirements:

- Cardboard recycling is important and we are willing to try it.
- Don't hold the user accountable for a recycling container misused by others.
- Tier the recycling requirements by the company's size so its affordable.
- Create a stepping stone process to go from 0 to 100% over time.
- Provide recognition for effort.
- Cost to inspect and enforce should be neutral.
- Secure and provide equipment when necessary prior to mandating.
- Have a trial period for learning and adapting.
- Incentivize companies to haul containers during off-hours or days.
- Don't make recycling mandatory, have an opt out process.

Next step was to validate learning take-aways from all the groups and interviews. This required a larger sample population to query, and at the same time, request anything extra. The survey was emailed to a number of companies, firms, and government officials with the same precept:

> "Our goal is to increase construction related cardboard recycling to 100%."

The participants were asked to rank the importance of the key needs and requirements and then add any thoughts/suggestions. This email generated several replies and calls primarily from government officials asking why they weren't "enacting and mandating" like they were accustomed to.

The team analyzed the information from the survey which registered no surprises. The only additional item received that was not previously captured from the interviews was related to ensuring county facilities were kept abreast of the potential incoming material.

Armed with the "real needs" from their respective populations, the team was ready to start designing a process that would answer or mitigate the requirements brought up. Using a Failure Mode and Effect Analysis spreadsheet (while inviting some former interviewees to the brainstorm session), they finalized the list to be used in the design, and an eventual draft of the ordinance. Some of the included items featured:

- Ramp up from 0 to 100% (goal) in 5 years.
- Residential Contractors building 5 or more homes in a single site will be required to participate.
- The county will "award" a Green Construction Site or a Green Event certificate and logo to be displayed by the builder or by the event programming.
- Haulers will be paid to pick up weekend event recycling at a slight premium.

The team then created process maps for deploying, operating, and maintaining such a program for both builders and special events. The processes included all responsible and accountable parties, what they are expected to do, and where in the process they interact. A communication plan is drafted together with a pilot test plan to launch the first version of the process.

Reaching out to some of the same builders and event coordinators, a call is made to a small number of volunteers to the program, outlining the benefits including how the county will market and advertise the volunteers to the program to the general public. To their astonishment, they received more replies to participate than they had expected. As such, they decided to expand the pilot by staggering start dates. That way, each subsequent pilot would accommodate the lessons learned from their predecessors.

A lot of things went wrong during the first pilot. However,

limiting the pilot to a few participants, and staggering future pilot participants, did allow for solutions to be worked out between pilots, making each iteration a better experience for all.

At one point, one of the issues encountered came from a builder, whose recycling container was being filled faster than expected. A quick look at the container showed that residents were using the container for their own cardboard depository, mostly for small appliances purchased in typical, new home environments. The builder was upset about it, but during discussion with the county team someone asked, "where do you think that cardboard used to go before they found your container?" They all answered in unison -
"The garbage!"

"So, we're helping achieve our goal then, right? I realize it's an added expense, but if you can figure out a way to recover it.... If not come back to us and we will work out a deal" commented the county team leader.

The builder decided to try a new concept, add $50 to the price of a home or lot, and call it "New Home Cardboard Recycling Initiative," during the sell process their salesforce would tell prospects, "this big cardboard recycling bin is for you and your neighbors to bring us all your cardboard after your residential bin is full. It's a convenience we offer all members of the subdivision to help reduce waste to the landfill." They registered zero complaints, and more than a dozen accolades for the services, especially since it was unique, and they were the only builder doing it. Situation resolved.

After all the pilots were completed, new issues were identified, processes refined, and the team provided the documentation to the attorneys to be drafted into an ordinance. It was at this time that something funny happened. Builders were calling in to the department, and eventually the county commissioners, with messages of, "hurry up and pass the ordinance, what's the hold up?" They wanted the "green" info on their literature, they wanted to continue the pilots!

The ordinance was drafted and sent for review. The most common commentary was, "the language is too difficult to follow, can you add the process maps like you did in the pilot? Anyone can follow those..." So, the county added the process maps to show how the ordinance would work, sent it to the commissioners, and it was voted in immediately.

Now, who would have thought that.

2. MANUFACTURING OVERPROCESSING

Introduction:

Many firms with a high percentage of fixed costs mistakenly think LEAN Six Sigma is unable to measurably improve operational profitability. While large fixed cost operations face distinct challenges compared to those with high variable costs, if approached with the right mindset, LEAN Six Sigma can still provide a significant financial benefit. But to obtain these benefits organizations need to take a more holistic approach to costs and be willing to challenge their current thinking.

Background:

X Company manufactures products for Y industry. Ten years ago, Y industry was experiencing strong year over year growth. To meet this demand, X expanded their capacity to match the expected growth in the market. In order to maximize productivity, X stressed automation and eventually purchased 5, Z machines to produce their product.

Additionally, they promoted heavily from within the organization, concentrating on individuals who proved they could meet or exceed production goals. Five years ago however Y industry began to soften. X was still able to run near maximum capacity, but their backlog of orders was lower than what they had become accustomed to. Three years ago, Y industry really started to contract. X believed they had the financial resources to weather the downturn by eliminating overtime (to operate a 3rd shift) and other minor operational changes.

However, management has now determined it will likely take many years for the industry to fully rebound. To make matters worse, X still has the PP&E aligned to the demand of the market 5 years ago, and the cost of the PP&E is hefty. The only good news is they are no longer having any trouble meeting their deliveries! In fact, most of their orders are shipped out well before their deadline.

Present Day:

Glenn, VP of Operations, was glancing around his office, reminiscing of the days when demand was strong and growing. A binder then caught his attention, one he had received over 8 years ago when the company had considered implementing a LEAN Six Sigma program. They ultimately decided against it as they didn't see much value. After all, they were generating record profits.

Well, those profits have slowed so Glenn decided to thumb through the binder.

When he got to the section discussing "waste" he really started thinking. A well-known goal of LEAN Six Sigma is removing waste from the system to thereby improve overall profitability. But most of the examples discussed in the book were in environments with significant variable costs. If you can identify the waste in these organizations, extracting the cost is relatively easy.

But X had a high fixed cost structure. Even if he were able to identify the waste, how can you remove significant fixed costs? He didn't have an answer but thought a good first step would be to see if he could identify the waste that was already evident and go from there.

Reading about LEAN Six Sigma made Glenn's head hurt. He decided to take a walk to clear his mind, and the best place to get some air was on the loading dock at the back of the plant.

He arrived at the plant just in time to see Pat, the Platform Manager, closing the doors of a trailer with a major customer's order on board. Pat was commenting that the order was being delivered to the customer a week and a half early. That should make them happy and, in this environment, keeping customers happy was everyone's top priority!

Glenn told Pat he was doing an excellent job and thanked him for his hard work. But privately Glenn was wondering if what Pat said was actually true.

> "Was shipping the product early to the customer really going to make them happy?"

Glenn thought back to the LEAN Six Sigma binder, and the category of waste called "Inventory." By shipping early did X just create additional waste in their customer's system? Was the customer even prepared to receive the delivery of inventory they hadn't planned on?

Now, X would take early shipments from their suppliers, but with the reduced demand, they had the space in their climate-controlled warehouse to accommodate it. Therefore, the excess inventory wasn't a problem. But did their customer have the extra space?

On his way back to his office Glenn passed by the Z machines. They really were amazing pieces of equipment. Each machine was about the size of a 3-bedroom house. When they were purchased they were truly state of the art. They had a few years on them by now, but X did an excellent job of spreading out demand. In fact, the latest weekly dashboard showed all the machines had very similar production.

Management had been reluctant to purchase the machines because they were afraid the large amounts of annual depreciation would hurt their P&L. However, their accountants said they could depreciate the machines based on units of output they produced, and this ability to marginalize the expense on the P&L helped to seal the deal.

It turns out depreciating the machines based on output really made a difference in the new environment. If a machine wasn't running, it wasn't costing X anything. Some days all 5 machines were in operation, but other days only a single machine may run.

The scheduler did a good job. Although the machine only required 2 people to operate it, she always tried to reduce the total amount of man-hours paid during a given operation. Because they were a union shop, once someone started working a shift they were paid the entire shift. Therefore, she didn't schedule a machine until she was sure it would be needed for the whole shift.

As Glenn continued back to his office he had waste on his mind. Where was it exactly? They certainly weren't overproducing. There were no finished goods inventory since they shipped the finished goods as soon as the orders were complete.

He knew it helped to think of waste in terms of dollars. So, the fact some of the machines were waiting at times didn't seem to matter. There was no impact to the P&L as long as they weren't operating. Plus, at times, all of the machines were needed.

The next morning Glenn was called out to the platform. For the first time anyone could remember a customer had refused to accept a shipment. They told the truck driver to come back in a week and a half when they had requested delivery. Glenn contacted the customer who proceeded to tell him all the trouble X causes when they ship their product ahead of time. In the past the customer had been able to find a place to store the materiel, but doing so made moving around the warehouse harder and possibly dangerous. In addition, the excess inventory required handling, which resulted in some damage. Plus, they didn't want to carry the excess inventory on their balance sheet.

Glenn couldn't believe what he was hearing. While X thought they were providing additional value, they were actually hurting their customer's operation. Thinking back to his Six Sigma binder, Glenn thought this had to be related to over-processing.

Over-processing is incurring an unnecessary expense to provide something to the customer he/she is unwilling to pay for (doesn't meet any need). In other words, it is an uncompensated cost. X thought delivering early and not getting compensated for it was actually making the customer happy. In this case it was doing the exact opposite!

But, why were they delivering early? Glenn was unaware of any operational guideline that required them to ship early. The managers were brought up in an environment of heavy demand, and remember when we mentioned that X liked to promote from within? These folks had come up in the organization when X was constantly struggling to meet the delivery requirements and pushed production as quickly as possible. The individuals who were successful in pushing the production were the ones who were promoted.

But Glenn was now starting to understand the company was not really tracking "on-time," instead they were reporting "in-time." A shipment arriving to the customer when they ordered it to arrive was categorized as "on-time." A shipment that arrives at the customer prior to when they want it is "early." Perhaps their metric needed to be changed.

It seemed as if shipping orders early met part of the definition of over- processing. They thought they were providing a "benefit" (early shipment) and not charging the customer. But where was the extra cost?

As he walked back to his office he passed the Z machines. Only one was actually in use at the moment. He thought there must be some waste in the fact only 1 of the 5 machines was in operation. But he knew the costs on the P&L (depreciation) were tied directly to production.

Glenn gazed at the incredible size of the machine and started wondering what other costs were associated with simply owning and caring for one of the Zs. He made a quick list:

- Interest – when they purchased the machines they borrowed the funds.
- Maintenance – some was performed based on volume, but most was performed at established intervals of time.
- People - X had to ensure enough crews were trained and available in case they decided to run all 5 machines.
- Plant Space – he wasn't sure how to quantify this, but they sure took up a lot of space in the plant. That must cost something, somewhere.

Glenn needed to talk with the finance department about how to quantify the potential costs associated with the list he had created.

Later that day Glenn and his management team agreed to change their operating metric to shipments "on-time" versus "in-time." This should reduce the over-processing issue they had (early shipment) and keep the customers happy.

About a week later Glenn was called out to the plant floor. When he arrived, he was amazed to see a huge quantity of finished product stacked and waiting for shipment. There was so much of the product the people working on the platform could barely move their forklifts around. It had become so unsafe that two forklifts collided due to poor visibility.

Glenn quickly realized that not shipping the finished product hadn't removed waste from the system; it had simply converted one form of waste (over-processing) to another form (inventory). In fact, X had literally transferred the problem the customer was having to its own facility.

Everyone understood the company could not operate like this. They would either have to store the finished product somewhere else, or come up with a plan to eliminate the excess inventory. From his Six Sigma binder Glenn knew the best option was to eliminate the inventory. But the only way to do that was not to produce it in the first place until it was ready to ship.

He went back and looked at the prior week's operating dashboard to try and understand the utilization of each of the Z machines. Every week the dashboard shows how much each machine produces. The previous week each machine produced roughly the same amount. Yet, the report did not show how much could have been produced.

Glenn decided to ask the operations manager why the metric was shown this way. The response he received was that the number was calculated to determine the depreciation for the period. Since the number was already available they decided to use it - no point reinventing the wheel.

He dug out some dashboards from 5 years earlier and was amazed to see the current weekly production was barely half of what the machines had produced then. How come nobody on the management team ever noticed this, or if they did, never mentioned it?

Some changes were in the works ...

Actions:

Up first, Glenn roped off 2 of the Z machines and declared them unusable. He wasn't sure how X would be able to operate with only 3 machines, but his data told him they could. He knew it would take discipline to enforce this, so he actually considered making the machines non-workable. Luckily it never came to that.

Reducing the available the capacity required the operations team to keep the remaining 3 machines in operation. In other words, X could no longer afford to have its remaining machines idle, or waiting. "Waiting" is another form of waste LEAN Six Sigma tries to identify and reduce.

Thus, they redesigned the end-to-end operation around the goal of keeping the 3 available machines in use. The work encompassed an assessment of the entire process from order receipt through shipping. It was hard work, but after few months the new process was working without any major issues.

They also included their own suppliers. By including them in the assessment, they were able to better match the receipt of goods to production. They no longer received supplies early and were able to reduce their materials inventory.

When management and the employees finally proved they

could operate with only 3 machines, X decided to get rid of the other 2 machines. Eventually they were sold to a company in South America for their remaining book value. This removed significant interest expense.

X was also able to reduce some maintenance expense related to simply owning the excess machines and reduce the amount of people they needed to keep trained for those times when they used all 5 machines.

The climate-controlled warehouse was shut down and the space formerly occupied by the Z machines was used instead. This reduced the utilities expense associated with heating and cooling the warehouse. By storing the materials near the Z machines, they also reduced some costs associated with moving the materials from their warehouse to production (transportation).

Lastly, X began tracking production on a control chart instead of simply reporting the current week's total output. This way changes in the levels of production (good or bad) would be more visible to management.

Lessons:

If your business environment has changed significantly, yet your operations have not, you probably have an opportunity for improvement. X continued to operate in the environment with reduced demand the same way they operated when it was strong. Never under estimate the power of inertia!

Many times, operations are run in such a way that the true waste is hidden. By shipping early and spreading the output among the 5 Z machines, it was harder to identify the waste within X's production process.

In a fixed cost environment, the actual cost of waste may be harder to identify and remove. However, even if you can't remove all of it, you should still try to remove as much as possible. Creativity and the ability to think holistically will be important skills among your finance support.

Use control charts to report critical information. Nobody noticed the dramatic reduction in production because they simply reported the current week's production without any reference point. Control charts provide the required context in addition to using established rules for interpretation.

3. SALES IS NOT A PROCESS

Introduction:

You can't formalize sales, right? Sales is not a process, right? Sales is all about the art, the ability to connect with someone and separate them from their money. Well... contrary many old stories, there might be a process in sales, a methodology that, created by those who are successful and have the right frame of mind, can be transposed to others. Sales people do have a certain aptitude and willingness to engage others, as well as a high resistance to rejection. They have to, otherwise sales would never occur. We are not all selling iPhones, so let's look at a story of mortgage sales.

Background:

Banks are big and this one was no exception. With branches across the U.S., they had an audacious goal – double their mortgage originations. Well, that's a clear challenge if there ever was one. Ramping up mortgage originations can be achieved in a variety of ways. An internal sales force is one, but this can be pricey mainly due to compensation systems. Another thought –

utilizing a tunable channel of brokerage firms which are managed by Account Executives. These folks are supervised by Sales Executives and work with brokers to entice them to originate loans into the bank's system. The brokers are compensated for each loan that is sent to the bank, and the Account Executives are in turn compensated for each loan originated (after the loan is funded).

Account Executives are divided regionally, and occasionally engage in small skirmishes when territories are crossed. Think Crips vs Bloods, but in Audis, khakis and Banana Republic blazers. All jokes aside, it can be a rough environment where Account Executives compete for broker favors, with each brokerage firm representing a multitude of banks and financial institutions, all clamoring for the broker to send the customer loan their way.

Realtors, who tend to have a significant amount of influence on who their client applies for a mortgage with, have their own experience or preferences and are often not afraid to impart that information to their client. It's rather common to hear:

"I had a client go with ____ and it took over 4 months for them to respond."

"It's a free world, do what you want, but I would never recommend them."

"Trust me, call Joanne at _____, she'll take care of you."

Now that you've got some background information, let's get the meat of this puppy.

Actions:

"Lean Six Sigma for sales? You must be insane." Couple that with a dusting of sarcasm and that was the reaction of the Executive Vice

President for Sales when the team approached him asking him about this project. Fortunately for the bank, the head of the mortgage unit was up on Six Sigma and as such, willing to give it a try. Both guys had been raised in the mystique that people in sales are unique, like those lizard aliens that look like you and I, but are well – lizard aliens. Outfitted with secret weapons, it's useless to try and step into their world.

But the good news is, the reaction we received instead was, "Why not, the worst thing that could happen is we prove this Six Sigma stuff needs to stay in back office operations, and best case, we increase sales. Let's do it, assemble the team."

And just like that, we were off. A team was put together - "subject matter experts" (SME in industry jargon), long-term mortgage operators, and a Lean Six Sigma Master Black Belt.

Next step, the proverbial kickoff! Every project starts with one, right, and this one was no exception. And like many meetings at the bank, it had no agenda. How refreshing, just a conference room filled with egos. Variants of the following conversations could be heard throughout …

SME1: "We're tasked with doubling sales."

SME2: "How do we do that?"

SME1: "Jim, we know how to do that, we sell, we're lizard aliens, all we have to do is work the realtors."

SME3: "Exactly, we've done this before, what we really need to do is reestablish our realtor appreciation program"

SME1: "Right, and we can do it quickly, we just need leadership to agree to the funds and then we're off."

But amidst all the noise there was another voice in the group, a lone wolf emerging from the shadows.

"What kind of sales are we doubling?"

The room fell silent. Who was this masked (he wasn't masked, but it sounds more dramatic, right) figure daring to opine on this sacred subject.

The Master Black Belt stood up, "Are we looking at doubling home purchase types of sales? Are these the ones that are most available in the market? What about refinances? Do realtors get involved in those too?"

Good lord, even the SMEs had to admit these were some decent questions. And since there were no answers, the Master Black Belt continued, "Are sales at the same level in all our regions? Can we learn from areas where sales are high and sales opportunity low? Do we know what kind of brokers tend to give us more loans, what is their motivation?"

The Master Black Belt had their attention, and just like that the SMEs began to come up with answers, mostly half-ass junk they had heard over the water cooler, but in reality, no one really knew. It was then the job of the Master Black Belt to convince them.

"Why don't we list all things we want to know and need to know on the white board, and then see how we can get some answers to validate all the knowledge you have acquired."

Questions were gathered, and the team started to work through the goal statement. As they worked it through the SMEs quickly realized that no, realtors do not influence refinance mortgages all that much. And yes, 68% of the volume in the market was indeed refinance. Taking this into account, <u>they would have missed 68% of the market had they gone forward with the original idea.</u>

Data-crunch and analysis time:

- No, there was no correlation between volumes and regions.

- Yes, some geographical areas are more prone to refinance than purchase loans.

- Yes, the type of broker, segmented by their volume, can have a statistically significant effect on market share.

- High producing Account Executives do have a track record and low production variation.

- Low producing Account Executives also do have a trend and low production variation.

- High and low producing Account Executives could be in the same area, calling on different brokers.

- Brokers seem to be motivated by their fee and ease of not only boarding the loan, but obtaining information about the loan for their client

As the data poured in the team experienced a collective "ah-hah" moment - the volume was available, it was simply going elsewhere.

The Master Black Belt then drove the team to the ask, "what are the Account Executives doing, and how are those that succeed different from those who do not?"

It was not a question of process, since it had been established earlier on that, "everyone knows sales people don't follow a process, they are lizard aliens." Still, the Master Black Belt knew that they could get there by simply avoiding the trigger words that shut the communication of information down. The team was convinced to select various Account Executives from the data. The selection criteria were two-fold: origination volume and consistency. Looking at extremes, they found high production Account Executives as well as low producing ones that have been consistently high and low.

The next step was to bring them all together in one place. New York, Chicago, San Francisco, Seattle – nope, Cleveland. But of course, Cleveland, a one day meeting, fly in and fly out. The bank leaders were impressed with the information the project had generated and agreed to fund the exercise. Even better, the Account Executives were thrilled to take part. Most assumed they would view a day in Cleveland as a bigger waste of time than another Star Trek remake, but just the opposite:

> "Sure, it's about time we do something like this."

The magical day arrived with a turnout of 21 Account Executives from every region of the bank. The Master Black Belt started it off by explaining progress to date, insight the team had gained, and the information that could be used by the Account Executives to further their respective client bases. They then quickly ran through expectations:

> "Guys, what we want from you is your story, tell us what you do and how you do it. We're not looking for secret handshakes, just what you do with brokers on a daily or weekly basis."

Next step was to separate the two groups, and have the Master Black Belt float between the two to observe and ask questions. A key point, he explained to facilitators, was never to use the word process in the rooms. The goal here was to understand what it is they do.

Shortly after the sessions started, the Master Black Belt observed a failure mode. The Account Executives started to talk among themselves as to what they do, and how they do it in general terms. The SME's then began to correct them with statements like, "you don't do that, do you? I mean, when I was in your job we did it ..."

Not good, as old war stories were not the reason the group was flown out in the first place. The SME's were quietly summoned to the hallway and reminded of the ground rules:

"Don't tell them what to do, only ask clarifying questions if you want, but let them tell you what they do and why."

Ground rules re-established, the SME's entered the rooms again and continued to gather information. With this new level of clarity, another pattern emerged. The group of high volume, high performing Account Executives where agreeing to what they do, from the time they get up in the morning to the time they go to bed – totally in sync. They had different terminology, but in the end, in a matter of a couple of hours, they all agreed to what they do in a fairly consistent manner. The room with the lower performing Account Executives however were still arguing as to how they even contact a broker.

The level of discussion and disagreement in the lower performing group was clearly visible, and the biggest complaint was along the lines of:

"Well, you see, brokers don't want to deal with us, they hate the bank and having to use our system."

This was particularly interesting, as brokers were clearly key cogs to success here, so what were the high-performing Account Executives doing different? Did they have pre-established relationships with brokers?

The Master Black Belt returned to the high-performing room and asked the million dollar questions, "How do you guys get into the broker's offices? How do you secure the meeting and keep them entertained long enough to teach them how to board loans onto the system?" The answer was literally too simple to believe. Amidst a roar of laughter, the group, nearly in unison, burst out, "That's the easy part!"

They explained, "All you have to do is meet the receptionist, go in person, introduce yourself, and ask what the firm's favorite lunch place is. Then you set up a free lunch to be delivered from that place to the firm, and on that day, you have an hour to get to know them, and teach them the boarding system so they can casually eat, watch it, and try it out."

Amazingly enough, every single one had the same or similar tactic. The Master Black Belt returned to the lower performing room and inquired as to who had done the same.

> "Well, we used to do that, a long time ago, but the bank no longer reimburses us, so we stopped doing it."

A bit confused, the Black Belt returned to the high-performers to see if this was the case. Indeed, it was, but what the high-performers had realized over time was while a two to three hundred dollar lunch is a set-back in the short-term, it wasn't so bad if they could secure twenty thousand dollars two months later. With that said however, the take-home salary of lower performing Account Executives ranges from $44,000 to $65,000 a year. The higher performers, all of them, average just about $1 million. You want to buy the broker's lunch now?

The team now had the improvement information, ranging from the data analysis, and the various "voices" of customer efforts, to create process changes and guidelines that will help to increase origination volumes across the bank's key markets. The goal was to double that number, and certain markets were analyzed and selected based on those market's ability to mimic the rest of the nation. One <u>key addition</u> in this pilot was the inclusion of funds to reimburse Account Executives for buying lunch for a broker's office while introducing the boarding system. Those markets and Account Executives who took advantage of the pilot did not double their volume however, rather they <u>tripled or in some cases quadrupled</u> their origination volumes. After the pilot was complete, most Account Executives decided to continue to fund the lunch by themselves and follow the process and guidelines.

The process and guidelines were fine-tuned after the pilot, adjusted to local market nuances, and rolled out across the bank. Volumes began to increase at a steady pace as the rollout continued. Volume really began to have an impact within the loan fulfillment centers, where leadership had heard about the sales initiative, but initially thought it was a lot of hot air. Now they were desperate for some relief, and decided to call one of those Master Black Belts to see what they could do. But that our friends, is a story for another day ...

4. THE MARCHING BAND

Background

Not every situation we can apply Lean Six Sigma to needs to be a drawn out project, sponsored by leaders to solve a significant issue. Often times, defining the problem via the use of simple questions to arrive at the root cause, then creating and testing a new process, and lastly, adopting it, can be a matter of a couple of days. This applies to any environment, including of all things a High School Marching Band uniform fitting process.

You remember the last time you were in a marching band uniform fitting, right? It was just yesterday, but of course! Well, if your memory escapes you, band uniform fitting is a major deal in the marching world. It can affect how one marches, moves, holds an instrument, and yes, how they look and feel. But in a real marching band competition, points can be lost due to ill-fitting uniforms. It's an unjust world, we know.

Situation

Marching band uniforms come in sets - pants and jackets. When purchased from manufacturers, the set arrives matched to the school. The sizes are such that - a 36 inch waist pant comes matched to a 36 inch chest jacket. Pants and jackets stay together as they were purchased, because that's the way it has always been done. The process is to have the marcher try on the uniform closest to his/her size, and if it fits, they keep it. The pants may be too large, the jacket too small, or vice versa. There is always a compromise, because that's the way it's always been done.

The only change permitted in fact is the hemming of the pant legs. This is to protect them from shredding, so they are shortened. But if the pants are too short, they cannot bet let out.

Root cause

A new marching volunteer enters the scene. Bad news, this person is familiar with Lean Six Sigma and asks rather innocently, "why are the uniforms so badly matched?"

Let's call this person Volunteer 1 (V1). V2 is an old timer, and the ensuing conversation went like this:

V1 – It's great to meet you V2. Looking forward to collaborating where I can. But to start out, I've noticed the uniforms fit really unevenly. What's the deal?
V2 – Thanks again for coming on, V1. Regarding the uniforms, unfortunately that's the best we can do, they are matched units.
V1 – What does that mean, matched?
V2 – That's how they arrive, we keep them that way, and if they fit well enough, we let it go.
V1 – But they don't fit, look how bad these are, can we fit them separate? Pants, then jackets?
V2 – No, we can't. They have a serial number, and we use that number for the kid assigned the uniform. When we dry clean the uniforms, once a year, the dry cleaner gives us tags to put on the uniforms. When we get them back, we use the dry cleaner tag to ensure the right kid gets the right uniform.
V1 – So we do this only because of the dry cleaner tags, and we do that only once a year, the rest of the season the kids look like Bozo the Clown? (Ok, V1 didn't say that, after all it's the first

couple days and all. But you get the picture)

V1 – Who is the dry cleaner? How do we track the kid's uniform numbers to dry cleaner tags?

V2 – Each kid has an index card with their name, uniform number and dry cleaner tag number. Its Triple A Dry Cleaners.

V1 – So the only reason to keep the uniforms together is for the dry cleaner and return process? Could the dry cleaners give us 300 tags, instead of 150 for the uniforms, and we record the tag for the pants, and the tag for the jacket in the same index card for each marcher?

V2 – We don't do it that way.

V1 – I know, but can they do it?

V2 – Not sure, they would probably charge more for separate piece cleaning versus single uniforms. Can't do it.

At this time, V1 goes outside to make a phone call, and returns with a smile:

V1 – Guess what, I called Triple A, they charge more for the uniform set versus separate because they have to clean and track together. But they would be happy to give us extra tags and we will pay $2.50 less per uniform if we give them separate units - pants and jackets. Then we can fit all the kids with pants and jackets that actually fit. The cleaners also said if we give them an inseam number for the pant legs, they will trim the pants, free of charge!

V2 was not amused. Stuck in the past, the response was -

V2 – Sounds interesting, but not sure we can do all that.

V1 – Why not? Let's ask the Band Director, I'm sure he can use a $375 savings in the budget and better fitting uniforms.

V2 – I guess we can try it, will be tricky.

V1 – Let's do the first 15 kids this way and see how it goes.

V2 – (Smoke fuming from her ears but with a fake Southern smile) Sure, bless your heart, let's try it.

V1 – Hey, next year, we can even email kids a uniform sheet, asking for pants and jacket sizes, and we can come here before they start, put together the uniforms they selected ahead of time, so we don't have to spend time looking for pants and jackets when they are being fitted.

V2 – Don't know, we have never done that ...

Interim Fixes

The process was implemented:

- Obtain marcher pants size
- Retrieve pants of that size or closest available to try on
- Record pant serial number in marcher index card
- Record pant length adjustment for dry cleaner to adjust
- Obtain marcher jacket size
- Retrieve jacket of that size or closest available to try on
- Record jacket serial number in marcher index card

There are now 2 additional pieces of information in the index card, and the process went like clockwork for the first 15 marchers. The volunteers would process 15 to 20 marchers per day and they finished in less than 90 minutes with the new process on the first 15.

Solution

The rest of the marchers were asked to continue visiting the uniform room, and by the second day, they were done with the uniforms ready for dry cleaner tags. The tags were attached and delivered to the dry cleaners together with the tag/adjustment needed for any of the pants. The cleaner was happy to get even more time to do the pant legs, 6 extra days, and the uniforms were returned with ample time for the marchers to perform one final try. Only 3 of the 67 requiring pant adjustments had to be redone.

So, what did we end up with:

- A faster process …
- that was less costly …
- with happier "end users" …
- with happier "customers" …
- with a better partnership with the "supplier" …
- and an unhappy old-timer who doesn't like change.

How often do you hear in your business, "we don't do it that way here." That phrase is a productivity killer. Ask "WHY?" enough times, get to the root cause, and then realize if it makes sense or not.

5. THE HEAT DID IT

Introduction:

It's typical for us to seek and assign names or actions to cause and effect. "X" happened because of "Y," I know it did and if we can minimize "Y" we should be Ok. We're consistently trying to find the reason something happened. That's good in many cases, it separates us from every other species on the planet. Yet a sound hunch or a gut feeling isn't 100% reliable. A tested toolset is really what is needed as companies can spend an inordinate amount of resources based on faulty hunches. The following is a prime example, featuring some exotic settings and a couple Fortune 100 company leaders. Strap in!

Background:

Printing. It's been a long standing industry with great advancements and benefits to humanity. In today's standards, digital printing equipment, both personal and business, continues to evolve in complexity and quality. Z Corporation is an industry giant, with a long history of innovation in the science of printing and a leader among its peers. Like many large manufacturing companies, it is filled with engineers designing and testing new ideas and products, visionary leaders looking beyond the horizon for that next great break-through, and a strong manufacturing workforce with advanced knowledge on how to assemble quality products to be shipped and used anywhere in the world.

This story is about one small product, a personal or small office digital printer/copier/scanning device, capable of churning out over 20,000 prints from a single "cartridge" (the ink jets trembling in their boots), and an international market looking for a product to fill this niche. The product is made of two components: the printer body (machinery) and the cartridge. The latter is the only component that the owner of the machine can physically change, and it can be found in local retail stores. The cartridge design team works in close unison with the main machine designers to ensure for the flawless integration of the two.

Another group of individuals, the lead executives, are more sales and marketing oriented and focused on getting the product to the market tomorrow. In conjunction the engineers and technicians who create the designs and ideas continue to test as every cycle iteration creates new knowledge that advances the science. The lead executives and engineers/trainers create a healthy checks and balances - the product is not rushed to market half-baked, while also not overly delayed due to yet another technological tweak.

During the design and testing phases, prototypes are subjected to a high degree of scrutiny, including operations under extreme conditions such as hot and cold environments, humidity, and altitude to name a few. Field testing is also conducted to ensure the prototypes receive sufficient "real world" visibility coupled with feedback from would-be customers. At this stage in the process changes are brought forward to ensure the product will operate under any condition – during a Florida summer or a Maine winter day.

In this instance, the product launch was a giant success. Orders began to flood in it is so successful that Z Corp decided to private label the product for other manufacturers willing to sell it as their own brand. Volumes are robust, business leaders feel confident of the product's success, and plans are set in motion for upcoming variants and follow-up products.

Present Day:

Print cartridges are shipped in advance of the machines. The expectation is that for every machine sold, the client will go through 4 to 5 cartridges every 6 months. As such, a stock of cartridges at various distribution centers worldwide must be ready for future purchases. Some of these distribution centers are located in northern, cold climates, with others in tropical, hot zones. The latter is where problems began to appear ...

Manaus is a thriving city in center-north, Brazil located along the mighty Amazon river. With fast and efficient air service to major centers throughout South America, it is a prime location for business distribution. Z Corp set up a distribution center is this muggy city located close to the equator, and the principal warehouse is ventilated, but not air conditioned. While temperatures, compared to Florida or California for instance, can be roughly the same, it was in Manaus where a customer cartridge failed first.

The customer didn't know what happened, they only knew "the thing was broken." It was returned to Z Corp under a warranty failure, and once the failed cartridge arrived at the factory a team of engineers began the process of taking it apart to examine the failure. At this stage in the life of the product, Z Corp had received very few failed units. Not surprisingly, this one confounded the engineers. There are two metal blades, glued together to create friction, and the they were separated at the glue joint. This was a first for everyone and the team subsequently wrote up a findings report to present to management.

The interesting twist to this failure was the unit was dead on arrival to the client. There was no wear and tear as nothing was ever printed. The team asked Manaus warehouse personnel to randomly select similar units to be analyzed. At one point a higher executive opined:

"Brazil is hot, and Manaus is real hot. That's got to be it."

This understandably created a whirlwind of whispers and rumors. A week later, the rest of the sampled units arrived at Z Corp. They were tested and revealed that that the two metal blades had either a fully failed glue joint, or an impending failure in the works. The engineering team returned to management where the same higher executive felt vindicated:

"I told you, it's the heat, things are different down there."

This specific gentleman had been to Brazil prior on a site visit, and this of course made him an expert in the eyes of his peers. At the same time Z Corp had also started a Lean Six Sigma program, a no-nonsense methodological process designed to arrive at the root cause of issues following a path of empirical evidence. The head of the design department had come across one of these Six Sigma "masters" and remembered him asking if there was anything the program could do for him. The design head gave it some thought and decided to bring him aboard. A little while later the design head received a call from one of the manufacturing Vice Presidents regarding the heat/product issue. The design head asked for a couple days and promptly got on the line with the Six Sigma Master.

The next day he and the Black Belt sat down for coffee. The "feeling" that this was heat related caused the Black Belt to chuckle, "feelings are for Saturdays, beliefs are for Sundays. The rest of the week, we need to know." The Black Belt prepped his team, and now to the meat of this story.

Actions:

Over the next few hours the Black Belt:

1) Informed his boss about the project;
2) Wrote up the "charter";
3) Connected with the Manaus warehouse manager;
4) Swung by the Quality Control (QC) lab;
5) Picked up a few discarded units, and;
6) Drove to the meeting location and connected with the rest of the team.

These dudes are efficient!

The meeting started, and the Black Belt wrote on the white board:

"Two blades are getting separated on the glue joint. What do we know?"

A flurry of hands went up and discussion about heat, Manaus, snakes, you name it. The Black Belt interrupted, leading the room back to some grounded questions:

- What is the temperature of the warehouse in Manaus?
- Does the temperature vary by location in the warehouse?
- What about humidity, what is it?
- Did anyone check with the glue manufacturer for temperature controls?
- Where else is this problem happening?
- What is the strength of the glue joint at room temperature?
- What is the strength of the joint when heated?

- What is the life expectancy of the glue joint?
- Have the batches of glue differed during the manufacturing process?

The team was rendered mute, realizing how little they really knew. They had all heard the senior leader's cries of "the heat" and bought it immediately. But no one really knew anything. The Black Belt had seen this before and reassured the team that they would start compiling some empirical data and revert back.

When the Black Belt returned he was pushing a small cart with 7 print cartridges and what looked to be black tape. He asked the team to split the units to determine if there was glue failure. None of them did. He then informed them that the black tape had been measuring the temperature of these units in his car's trunk for the past few hours. It had peaked at 155 degrees F, yet no failures. How hot could Brazil actually be?

Next, the Black Belt whipped out an email string between himself and the Manaus warehouse manager where they had been monitoring the temperature at the warehouse - 135 degrees F. So, what was up here?

The Black Belt indicated more data was necessary, but obviously recalling all units in hot climates would clearly be a waste of resources. Over the next few days print cartridge samples began to arrive to the team to investigate. They arrived from Holland, Japan, and the United States. Some of these samples did have the impending glue joint failure, some did not, and some were fully failed. At this point the team and the Black Belt started to create a plan to visit the blade and glue assembly area, connect with the manufacturing team to see what was being measured, understand the overall process and potential trouble-spots, and investigate the actual glue and how it works. After mapping the assembly process, they devised a test plan to measure the strength of the glue joint under various conditions as well as interview the glue provider surrounding the properties of the glue.

The team tested the strength by pulling the two metals apart at various stages post-gluing - heating them up to 200 degrees F and cooling them to freezing temperature. They tested and measured various quantities of glue applied (from oozing to very little), and investigated methods for "cleaning" the metal before gluing. This data provided the first real body of knowledge as to how blade assembly behaved under changing conditions, and the results were not promising. The joint was indeed weak, and was weak in Manaus or in New York, it didn't matter. Temperature didn't matter.

It was time to report back to the senior leaders as to the findings and give them an update on actions taken. It's never fun nor gratifying telling senior leaders their snap judgements were just that – snap and without any basis. During the meeting senior leaders found it difficult to counter the facts and data presented. Some blustered on until the Vice President of Manufacturing interrupted:

"Do we want to allow this team to continue to figure out what is wrong and fix it with facts and data, or would you all rather shoot from the hip with feelings even though aimless action could cost us millions?"

A senior leader then responded, "that's fine, but I thought Six Sigma projects took months to close out." The Black Belt looked at the room with a smile:

"This will take one week, two at the most."

Cyanoacrylates. Run to the Dr. if this shows up. Just kidding, this was the type of glue being used. Since the data pointed to a weak glue joint, a conference call and eventual face to face meeting with the glue provider was imperative. The application, equipment, and final usage of the glue was discussed with the manufacturer's representative, who seemed divided between, "yeah, it should work," and, "not sure we are looking at the best use of the glue here." The best explanation (in layman's terms) was to imagine the cyanoacrylate as a single chain. Extremely strong, but if one link breaks, the bond is weakened.

"We are using the wrong glue." Not sure who said it first, but it was obvious. The manufacturer agreed, but stated it differently – "it's actually the right glue, just the wrong application." OK, either way, a correct one was needed. One of the glue manufacturer's chemists then said, "what you need for your application is a structural adhesive, not a cyanoacrylate." Bingo, was one of those available? Unfortunately, no, they didn't have one, but a quick call to the Supply Chain specialist at Z Corp headquarters yielded a few names and contacts. An overnight shipment was set up – let the experimentation begin.

The next day the team spent the time designing and setting up a series of experiments to measure the samples, and to test the ideas for improving the glue joint. Once the samples arrive the tests were conducted, including all the factors that could affect the joint strength. The Black Belt made sure high temperature was one of the factors since they knew senior leaders would hold on to their precious "feelings."

Here is where it gets interesting - the steel was breaking, tearing up, before the glue joint came apart. This was an improvement the team was definitely not expecting. Once they tested all the samples they called up the Supply Chain representative who recommended two suppliers based on past experience. Both supplier products would be qualified, and cost for their product as well as cost of the new glue dispensing and application equipment considered. That way Z Corp would have a primary supplier and backup supplier.

The last step for the Black Belt was to optimize the amount of adhesive and document the process to be followed together with an action plan should the process go awry. Also, a plan was put in place to test the glue joint and record the strength of the joint in a control chart and track the "normal" expectation of the adhesive. Another surprised awaited the team as not only was the amount of structural adhesive needed less than the cyanoacrylate, the cost of the dispensing equipment was approximately $2,500 compared to $38,000 for the high precision cyanoacrylate! Management tends to like surprises like this. The equipment was installed by the third week of the project and qualified for operations by the manufacturing team.

The Black Belt suggested a video of the glue joint testing be part of the next presentation to the senior leaders. During the meeting, the audience gasped when they heard the loud "clang" of the steel breaking when using the new adhesive, compared with the rather mild quiet slippage of the old glue joint. They were sold on the idea, and even voted to go along with the concept of manufacturing the blades and shipping them to the warehouses where the local personnel could replace them on-site and reseal the boxes. Yes, even in Manaus, avoiding a large cost of shipping and the larger print cartridges back and forth.

Lessons:

- It's easy to jump to conclusions when we see or hear "evidence" of what the cause of the problem is. Doing that without the facts can lead to excessive costs to an operation without addressing the true root cause of the problem.

- Lean Six Sigma projects do not have to take a long time to complete. Having a dedicated workforce trained as experts in the methodology will provide a company with the highest returns on investment compared to any other problem solving program.

• Managing by facts and data provides any organization with common ground and common purpose to achieve their goals in the most efficient and effective manner. By allowing the facts to test all thoughts and ideas, you can truly discern which factors do matter to the desired outcome of your product or service.

• Lean Six Sigma doesn't end when the solution has been found and tested. The solution is optimized to help minimize wasted resources - the process document and a plan to measure and control the new improved process to avoid backward slippage then must be implemented.

• Sometimes the solution to the problem is a lower cost solution than the current state. Lean Six Sigma is designed to find the lowest cost solution without scarifying quality. Keeping an open mind and asking many questions are, in the end, the best tools for any Lean Six Sigma practitioner.

6. TRADITIONAL MORTGAGE PROCESSING

Introduction:

The traditional, top-down management structure in most companies is driven by departmental or group inertia. That's the way it's always been, so why change it! Your typical mortgage processing firm will have processors led by a team leader, and led in turn by a Processing Leader. Underwriters have a similar structure, with hierarchies based on their own "specialty." Making an all too familiar baseball analogy, you'd have a team of pitchers, another team of catchers, another team of infielders and outfielders, etc. In reality we know they work in unison as a team to win.

But in most cases, our own organizational structures get in the way of winning. Ever heard this famous refrain when calling a company with questions ... "sorry, this department doesn't handle that ..." Let's shake this up a bit and see what happens.

Background:

The American Dream is home ownership. The plot of land, the apartment, the property with the old barn that we would like to own. Ownership typically involves the acquisition of a mortgage, a loan on the property that a financial lending institution would grant a qualified borrower. Mortgage fulfillment is two-fold: processing and underwriting. In processing, the processor takes the application from sales, reviews the information, and orders documentation (flood certification, appraisal, property title search, homeowner's insurance status, etc.). Processing also becomes the main point of contact for the borrower, as well as any other internal and external entities involved with the mortgage process. Processors have to juggle all these interactions and adhere to a number of metrics that management imposes on them, most related to things they have no control over.

The second phase actors, Underwriters, assess the property value (collateral) and the borrower's ability to repay the mortgage and their willingness to repay the loan. These are very important points to ensure that the bank manages risk appropriately while maximizing profits for their shareholders. Banks seek a profit, so bad loans equal less profit. Underwriters work with the borrower via the Loan Processor, as the Processor is the only person authorized to contact the borrower/client directly.

These are key positions in the process, requiring deep knowledge of the rules, laws, regulations, and Bank standards for assessing and processing loans correctly. Processors are trained for 3 months, including 4 weeks of classroom work (rules and systems), followed by 1-2 months of work training prior to being thrown into the fire on their own. Underwriter training takes a little less time, but the Bank assumes 2-3 months to arrive up to speed. Each then join a team of processors or underwriters and are managed by a more senior, team lead. Remember that baseball analogy? This is how it's done folks, how it's always been done.

Here's the issue - the Bank was losing market share as loans were simply taking too long to be approved. Average loan to funding time was a staggering 120 days, and management was painfully aware. Sales teams complained that not only prospective customers were being turned off, but key influencers like realtors were beginning to steer their clients away from the Bank. How do we cut into this 120 day nightmare? The Bank decided to consult professionals in the lean and six sigma group to investigate and return with solutions.

Actions:

The Lean Six Sigma (LSS) team was assembled and quickly went to work. Mortgage lending experts (part of the larger team) initially communicated that loans take in general 30-45 days to process, and the only reason they have skyrocketed to 120 was due to volume and the fact that management had decided not to hire any more loan processors or underwriters to absorb the extra demand. The LSS team diligently listened and took notes. Then on to their investigation.

First key question, what was the lending process and how much work is there to do that takes 45 days? Second, how much work does each processor and underwriter have? And third, how is the work managed, distributed, measured? The LSS team had questions 4, 5, 6, etc. loaded and ready, but decided to keep with the basics for the time being.

To begin, they needed to understand the process. After selecting one single processing site they dived into the minutia. By the time the information gathering was complete, they arrived at a conservative time of 3 hours of work per loan. Three hours! So, what is using up 120 days?

Here is where some complementary information comes into play. Processors request title searches, a function performed by external actors. They also need to receive appraisals on the property, which can take several days. Additionally, this is frequently a lot of information missing from the application and tracking down the borrower can be difficult.

Meanwhile, Underwriters are reviewing information that is incomplete and have to consistently send a list of issues to processors, who in turn have to contact borrowers again and again and again … you get the story. In fact, missing information is so common that underwriting team leads have created standard form letters to send to processors.

The LSS team pondered:

"Why aren't folks in sales being informed of the large amount of missing information? Are they aware of the reasons the loan decisions are being delayed? Is this information always the same?"

The processors and underwriter managers communicated that sales don't care really care since they get compensated when they submit the loan. The LSS reverted back to sales and their response couldn't have been more emphatic:

"We don't get paid until the loan is funded, not when we submit it. That's why we need your help in speeding this up!"

Read that again. This is communication and process, and the answer was in complete contrast with what the processing team thought. Sales obviously had a vested interest in getting it right the first time. With this said, the LSS team decided to create a measurement system, captured the main issues with the applications, and reverted back to sales force leadership for concurrence on a "refresher training" of their personnel. Since sales leadership also gained on funded loans, they quickly agreed.

Communication/training reduced the amount of deficient

information by 68% in the first month (post implementation). Over the next 3 months it plummeted 84%, remarkable to say the least.

Now, what you're probably wondering – what about the mortgage process and this 3 hours vs. 120 days thing? The team discovered that one of the shortest steps in the process was "contacting the customer," as processors agreed it was a brief, 10 minute conversation for the most part. What they didn't factor in however was that when the customer wasn't available, coupled with back and forth of voicemails, etc., days would pile up which quickly turned to weeks. Rules prevented the processor from leaving detailed messages on an answering machine. But to continue to call the same number at the same time of the day, expecting different results, was madness. More on this later ...

Another issue was communication, or lack thereof, between processors and underwriters. A typical problem was underwriters would receive incomplete information and instead of remedying it quickly via a phone call or in-person drop-in, they had form letters that they would pass on which would not always be received or returned on time.

The LSS team worked to identify the majority of the typical, missing information, add that to the application process (thereby securing it up front by the sales person) prior to submission. This resulted in information being captured 72% of the time during the sales application, and 100% within the first 3 days of when the application was submitted. This eliminated a large portion of the underwriting delays due to basic, missing information. This used to result in 100% rejection by underwriting - post implementation it dropped to 28%.

But the LSS team didn't stop there. Another interesting discovery was processors were engaged in activities that consumed a lot of their time. Perfect example, contacting the customer. This was something a "processor assistant" could do on a part-time, flexible basis. If the processor kept calling a customer at 3PM and they were never home, but couldn't call them at 8PM because the processor had already left work, this assistant could schedule their work day to arrive later and stay until 9PM to shore up the hard to reach customers. A simple yet effective solution to the problem is to have a lower cost, lower trained person who could contact customers later in the day and capture the critical information needed. As simple as this sounds, and the return of investment was less than 21 days, it took management a significant amount of time to debate the decision. But you see, Lean and Six Sigma is not about debating or who can make the best sounding argument, it's about facts, data, analysis, the realities of the business world instead of what we want to believe.

Then, it didn't take long after for the 120 days to tumble down to 45, then 30, then under 30 and held steady at the mid-20's for the entire rest of the high volume season. Word got out quickly, and market share followed.

7. APPLES AND ORANGES

How many times have you heard, "you can't compare those, it's like apples and oranges" from someone in your organization or a high paid "consultant" giving you advise? I know I did, so many times. And yes, it makes sense on the surface and is sounds like a catchy phrase. But what are we really saying is "hmm, I don't really know how to compare those two things". Yes, I said it, "don't know" is a not a phrase you hear often is it?

But when we are trying to make business decisions about processes, to meet changing and sometimes conflicting customer requirements, you have to disrupt the old happy go lucky thinking. Of course, you can compare dissimilar items, objects, requirements. It's easy to say you can't, hard to say "yes, let me look into it and get back to you".

So how do we compare apples and oranges?
- They are both fruit
- They are round, have a circumference
- Diameter
- Skin strength
- Skin depth
- Skin color
- Skin water absorption
- Number of seeds inside

- Position of the seeds
- Stem size
- Stem strength
- Weight
- Water content
- Juice yield
- Glycemic index
- Vitamins
- Fiber content

Tired yet? You get the point? I know many won't, they just can't see it, and that's okay. But next time you hear someone tell you "you can't compare that, apples and oranges", think "let's call Tactegra, they have an open mind and know how to do what I need".

8. LEFT HANDED PENCILS

Since the beginning of handwriting, left handed instruments have been overlooked. Number 2 pencils are no exception, designed for right handed individuals in mind. A charity in New York City decided to help lefties with free No. 2 pencil samples by reworking them as follow:
- Remove the rubber eraser from top of pencil
- Remove the metal band from top of pencil
- Sharpen the top of the pencil
- Re-insert the metal band and eraser on the opposite side

And voila'! You have created a left handed pencil by inverting a right handed pencil. The company will first give them away for free and eventually charge $0.10 each, sold to large corporations that are now shamed into ensuring they provide them for their employees.

Now, some of you are thinking "wait a minute, if the pencil is symmetrical, why invert it anyway, it's the same thing?!?!". Others might be thinking "it's about time, we lefties are left out, no pun intended". No doubt, there are tools designed for left handed persons, scissors come to mind as I have a few myself. But that's not what we are talking about here. Buckets of steam, left handed hammers, bags of electricity, four foot yardsticks, polka dot paint, AC batteries, and blinker fluid. We are talking about things that don't make sense, and you would never purchase or order.

But why do we succumb to similar things in the corporate world? The doubting Thomas mind we would use when a shop tries to sell us "blinker fluid" is jettisoned when we are back in the office, listening to a very persuasive and slick sales presentation about a large purchase of a new system component.

The salesperson is telling you the Initech model 1800 Appliance will solve the problem you need, and it is priced at $36,000 for the configuration you need. All the software is preloaded and all you need to do is drop it in place and boom-done. Sounds great, less work for you, and we always like turnkey less work systems. You and your staff smile and nod, deal is done, let's cut the P.O. and get this in quickly.

Next you need to secure a signature from your boss and bring the paperwork to their office. The boss scratches their nose and ask "Didn't we buy an Initech model 1800 last month, and wasn't it $12,800 or something like that?", you answer "well, yes, that was a server, this is an appliance, a dedicated appliance direct from Initech". "Oh, I see, what's the difference? "and you quickly reply, "Same exact box, but the software configuration is done at Initech, ready to go". "That must be some expensive software!", and you start thinking, wait, does this makes sense when the boss puts it that way? Time for a call to the salesperson.

It may sound unrealistic, but these kinds of situations do occur daily in the corporate world. We hear from our clients if we offer a certain flavor of a tool or solution set. We always ask "Why, what goal are you trying to achieve?", and often the response is that management is requesting it. The root cause of the strange request is more often than not simple; management sat down with a consulting firm and sold this great new solution set that has been proven many times to work on all business problems. As experts in the field we will research and look for this new, new thing only to find out is the same old, old thing repackaged and with a bright new label and "framework". In the world of process consulting, new ways of doing the same thing are created to problem solve, or invent innovative words like "solutioning" and the like. And in the quest for that "less work for us turnkey solution", many fall for the promise of the new new thing. But, unfortunately, not much is gained without challenging work and dedication.

New invented words with re-constituted products is nothing new, but we have seen a resurgence of these products, sometimes is the same old set of tools watered down, others are the same old tools pasted into a new framework. Our recommendation, don't jump in, don't buy the snake oil. Ask questions about it, or better yet, ask yourself how will this new solution actually helps me solve the problems that I am facing? Best case, call us, and we will research it for you and remove the layers of glitter to show you what it really is.

Don't take the easy road, it often leads you lower profits and more work for you!

ABOUT THE AUTHORS

Izzy Sanchez is a co-founder and Managing Partner of Tactegra, LLC. He has over 30 years improving and redesigning business processes in a variety of industries, all over the world, ranging from Manufacturing, Financial Services, and Insurance. A trained Engineer with advanced degrees in Mechanical Engineering, Izzy has experience in developing Continuous Improvement Programs from early strategy through mature implementation in multinational firms, including training creation, tailoring, delivery and certification at all levels.

Ian Cato is a co-founder and Managing Partner of Tactegra, LLC. With graduate degree in Finance and over 30 years of professional career, Ian has a proven track record of delivering profitable results through process transformation, continuous improvement, and program effectiveness. His true strength is in understanding the practical aspects of making changes to a company's way of doing business. His passion and integrity, combined with education and experience, make him a sought after consultant by companies wishing to align their priorities for success.

www.ingramcontent.com/pod-product-compliance
Lightning Source LLC
Chambersburg PA
CBHW030506220526
45464CB00006B/2673